Consciousness and Altered States

Exploring the Depths of Perception and Reality

Bienuel Tenio

Consciousness and Altered States
Exploring the Depths of Perception and Reality

Kindle Direct Publishing
410 Terry Avenue North
Seattle, WA 98109-5210
USA

Preface

In the vast expanse of human experience, consciousness remains one of the most enigmatic phenomena we encounter. It is the beacon of our awareness, the lens through which we perceive the world and ourselves. Yet, within the realm of consciousness lie uncharted territories—realms where perception is altered, where the boundaries between reality and imagination blur, and where the depths of the mind seem to unfurl in mysterious ways.

This book, "Consciousness and Altered States: Exploring the Depths of Perception and Reality," embarks on a journey into these unexplored dimensions of human consciousness. Through the lens of multidisciplinary inquiry, we delve into the myriad facets of altered states, from ancient shamanic rituals to innovative neuroscientific research, from the profound insights of meditative practices to the transformative potential of psychedelic experiences.

Chapter by chapter, we navigate through the labyrinth of consciousness, guided by the following waypoints:

In Chapter 1, we embark on our voyage with an Introduction to Consciousness and Altered States. Here, we lay the groundwork by defining consciousness and its altered states, setting the stage for our exploration into the depths of perception and reality.

Chapter 2, Historical Perspectives on Altered States, invites us to journey through time and space as we examine how altered states have manifested across cultures and civilizations. From ancient rituals to modern cultural movements, we uncover the diverse tapestry of human experiences with altered consciousness.

The journey continues in Chapter 3, where we venture into The Neuroscience of Consciousness. Here, we peer into the intricate workings of the brain, seeking to unravel the mysteries of consciousness and understand the neurobiological underpinnings of altered states.

In Chapter 4, Meditation and Mindfulness beckon us to explore the transformative power of inner contemplation. We delve into the practices of meditation and mindfulness, discovering their profound effects on consciousness and perception.

Chapter 5 invites us to probe the depths of Psychedelics and Altered Consciousness. From the ancient sacraments of Indigenous cultures to the resurgence of psychedelic research in the modern era, we explore the profound effects of psychedelic substances on perception, cognition, and consciousness itself.

Dreams and Lucid Dreaming take center stage in Chapter 6, where we unravel the mysteries of the subconscious mind. Through the realm of dreams, we uncover hidden truths and unlock the potential for lucid exploration of consciousness.

Chapter 7 beckons us to journey into the heart of Shamanic Traditions, where altered states serve as gateways to spiritual insight and healing. We delve into the rich tapestry of shamanic practices, exploring their cultural and spiritual significance across time and space.

In Chapter 8, we confront the interface between technology and consciousness. From virtual reality to brain-computer interfaces, we examine how technology shapes our perception of reality and alters the landscape of human consciousness.

The Philosophy of Consciousness takes center stage in Chapter 9, where we grapple with the profound questions of existence, reality, and the nature of consciousness itself. Through the lens of philosophy, we explore the metaphysical implications of altered states and their philosophical interpretations.

Finally, in Chapter 10, Integration and Future Directions, we chart a course for the integration of insights from altered states into everyday life. We confront ethical considerations and envision future avenues for exploration in the ever-expanding frontier of consciousness studies.

As we embark on this odyssey into the depths of human consciousness, may this book serve as a beacon of illumination, guiding us through the labyrinthine corridors of perception and reality. Let us embark on this journey together, with open minds and curious hearts, as we seek to unravel the mysteries of consciousness and explore the boundless realms of human experience.

<u>Table of Contents</u>

Chapter 1: Introduction to Consciousness and Altered States

Section 1: Defining Consciousness and Altered States.

To embark on a journey of understanding consciousness and altered states is to navigate through the intricate tapestry of human experience and perception. At its core, consciousness is the fundamental awareness of existence, the subjective experience of being alive and aware of oneself and the surrounding environment. It encompasses our thoughts, emotions, sensations, and perceptions, serving as the canvas upon which our reality is painted.

Defining consciousness proves to be a daunting task, for it resides at the intersection of philosophy, psychology, neuroscience, and spirituality. Philosophers have pondered its nature for centuries, grappling with questions of existence, identity, and the mind-body relationship. Psychologists seek to unravel its mysteries through empirical inquiry, studying its various dimensions and manifestations. Neuroscientists delve into the depths of the brain, unraveling the neural correlates of consciousness and exploring its biological underpinnings. Meanwhile, spiritual traditions offer profound insights into altered states of consciousness, transcending ordinary perception to access higher states of awareness and enlightenment.

Altered states of consciousness, on the other hand, represent deviations from the ordinary waking state of awareness. They encompass a spectrum of experiences ranging from meditation-induced states of deep tranquility to the profound shifts in perception induced by psychedelic substances. Altered states may also manifest during dreams, hypnosis, ecstatic rituals, or through profound spiritual experiences. In these states, the boundaries of perception blur, and the mind transcends its ordinary limitations, offering glimpses into deeper layers of reality.

Understanding altered states requires us to transcend conventional modes of perception and embrace the fluidity of consciousness. Rather than viewing consciousness as a static entity, we must recognize its dynamic nature, capable of traversing vast expanses of experience and perception. Altered states serve as portals into the depths of the human psyche, offering insights into the mysteries of existence and the nature of reality itself.

Section 2: Overview of the Significance of Exploring Perception and Reality.

The exploration of perception and reality lies at the heart of human inquiry, beckoning us to unravel the mysteries of existence and the nature of consciousness itself. At its essence, perception shapes our reality, filtering raw sensory data into meaningful experiences that inform our understanding of the world. Yet, beneath the surface of ordinary perception lie hidden realms of consciousness waiting to be explored.

The significance of exploring perception and reality extends far beyond academic inquiry; it touches upon the very fabric of human existence. By delving into the depths of consciousness, we gain profound insights into the nature of reality and our place within it. We come to understand that reality is not fixed and immutable but rather fluid and malleable, shaped by the subjective experiences of sentient beings.

Moreover, the exploration of altered states offers a unique opportunity to transcend the limitations of ordinary perception and access higher states of awareness. In altered states, the boundaries between self and other dissolve, giving rise to profound feelings of interconnectedness and unity with the cosmos. These transcendent experiences hold the potential to transform our understanding of ourselves and the world around us, opening doors to new possibilities and insights.

Furthermore, the study of altered states has far-reaching implications for fields ranging from psychology and neuroscience to spirituality and philosophy. By unraveling the mechanisms underlying altered states, we gain valuable insights into the workings of the human mind and the nature of consciousness itself. Such insights not only deepen our understanding of mental health and well-being but also pave the way for innovative approaches to therapy and self-exploration.

In essence, the exploration of consciousness and altered states is a journey of profound significance, inviting us to expand our horizons and embrace the mysteries of existence. It challenges us to question the nature of reality and our place within it, urging us to delve deeper into the recesses of consciousness in search of truth, meaning, and enlightenment.

As we embark on this journey together, may we approach it with open minds and curious hearts, ready to embrace the wonders that lie beyond the veil of ordinary perception. For in the exploration of consciousness and altered states, we may uncover truths that illuminate the very essence of our being and the universe itself.

Chapter 2: Historical Perspectives on Altered States

Section 1: Examination of Altered States Throughout History.

To delve into the historical perspectives on altered states is to embark on a voyage through the annals of human civilization, tracing the footsteps of our ancestors as they navigated the intricate terrain of consciousness and perception. From ancient rituals to modern cultural movements, the exploration of altered states has been woven into the fabric of human experience, leaving indelible imprints on the pages of history.

Ancient civilizations provide a rich tapestry of practices and rituals aimed at inducing altered states of consciousness. From the shamanic traditions of Indigenous cultures to the mystical rites of ancient mystics and sages, altered states served as gateways to transcendence and spiritual insight. In the depths of the Amazon rainforest, shamans journeyed into the realms of the spirit world through the use of sacred plants and visionary experiences, seeking guidance and healing from unseen forces. In the deserts of Egypt, initiates underwent transformative rituals in the pursuit of enlightenment and divine wisdom, transcending the confines of ordinary perception to commune with the gods.

Throughout the ages, altered states have played a pivotal role in shaping the course of human history, influencing art, religion, philosophy, and culture. In ancient Greece, the Eleusinian Mysteries offered initiates a glimpse into the mysteries of life and death, inviting them to partake in sacred rites and ceremonies that transcended the boundaries of ordinary consciousness. In medieval Europe, the ecstatic visions of mystics and saints inspired awe and reverence, serving as conduits for divine revelation and spiritual ecstasy.

The Renaissance witnessed a resurgence of interest in altered states, as scholars and philosophers delved into the depths of the human psyche in search of hidden truths and esoteric knowledge. From the visionary experiences of alchemists and magicians to the mystical insights of poets and artists, altered states served as catalysts for creative expression and intellectual inquiry, pushing the boundaries of human understanding beyond the constraints of reason and logic.

As we journey through the annals of history, we encounter a diverse tapestry of cultural practices and beliefs surrounding altered states of consciousness. From the mystical traditions of the East to the esoteric rites of the West, altered states have served as portals to the numinous realms of the soul, offering seekers glimpses into the mysteries of existence and the nature of reality itself.

Section 2: Cultural and Societal Perceptions of Altered States.

The cultural and societal perceptions of altered states offer a window into the collective psyche of humanity, reflecting the values, beliefs, and aspirations of diverse cultures and civilizations. Throughout history, altered states have been both revered and reviled, celebrated as pathways to enlightenment and condemned as pathways to madness and heresy.

In many Indigenous cultures, altered states are viewed as sacred and transformative experiences, integral to the fabric of communal life and spiritual practice. From the visionary rituals of the Native American peyote ceremonies to the ecstatic dances of African tribal traditions, altered states serve as conduits for healing, divination, and communion with the divine. Within these cultures, altered states are embraced as gifts from the gods, bestowing wisdom, insight, and guidance upon those who dare to venture into the realms of the unknown.

In contrast, Western societies have often viewed altered states with suspicion and fear, associating them with witchcraft, sorcery, and demonic possession. Throughout the Middle Ages, those who experienced altered states were often persecuted as heretics and witches, condemned to the flames of the Inquisition for daring to challenge the established order of church and state. Even in modern times, the stigma surrounding altered states persists, with psychedelic substances demonized as dangerous and addictive drugs, rather than revered as sacred sacraments capable of unlocking the mysteries of the mind.

The cultural and societal perceptions of altered states are deeply intertwined with broader social, political, and religious forces, reflecting the prevailing attitudes and ideologies of a given time and place. In some cultures, altered states are celebrated as gateways to spiritual enlightenment and self-discovery, while in others, they are condemned as threats to social order and moral authority.

As we navigate the complex terrain of cultural and societal perceptions, we are confronted with the profound diversity of human experience and belief. Altered states remind us of the boundless potential of the human mind and the infinite ways in which consciousness can manifest itself across time and space. They challenge us to question our assumptions and preconceptions, inviting us to embrace the mysteries of existence with humility, reverence, and awe.

In conclusion, the examination of altered states throughout history offers us a glimpse into the depths of human consciousness and the myriad ways in which it has been explored, celebrated, and understood. From the sacred rituals of Indigenous cultures to the visionary experiences of mystics and sages, altered states serve as portals to the numinous realms of the soul, inviting us to embark on a journey of self-discovery and transformation. As we journey through the annals of history, may we heed the wisdom of our ancestors and embrace the mysteries of existence with open minds and open hearts, for in the exploration of altered states, we may uncover truths that illuminate the very essence of our being and the universe itself.

Chapter 3: The Neuroscience of Consciousness

Section 1: Understanding the Brain Mechanisms Underlying Consciousness

The quest to understand consciousness has long captivated the minds of scientists, philosophers, and mystics alike. At the heart of this inquiry lies the enigmatic organ known as the brain—a three-pound marvel of evolutionary engineering that serves as the seat of human consciousness. Through the lens of neuroscience, we embark on a journey into the depths of the mind, seeking to unravel the intricate web of neural circuits and synaptic connections that give rise to the phenomenon of consciousness.

Central to our understanding of consciousness is the concept of neural integration—the dynamic interplay of neuronal activity across distributed networks within the brain. At any given moment, billions of neurons fire in synchrony, forming complex patterns of activity that underlie our thoughts, emotions, and perceptions. Through the process of synaptic transmission, information flows seamlessly between neurons, giving rise to the rich tapestry of subjective experience we know as consciousness.

Neuroscientists have identified a number of brain regions and networks that are critically involved in the generation and modulation of consciousness. The thalamus, often referred to as the "gateway to consciousness," serves as a relay station for sensory information, integrating signals from the external environment and transmitting them to higher cortical regions for processing. The prefrontal cortex, meanwhile, plays a key role in executive functions such as decision-making, self-awareness, and introspection—hallmarks of human consciousness.

Recent advances in neuroimaging techniques, such as functional magnetic resonance imaging (fMRI) and electroencephalography (EEG), have shed new light on the neural correlates of consciousness, allowing researchers to map patterns of brain activity associated with different states of awareness. Studies have shown that alterations in consciousness, such as those induced by anesthesia or sleep deprivation, are accompanied by changes in the functional connectivity of neural networks, highlighting the dynamic nature of consciousness and its susceptibility to external influences.

Yet, despite these advances, the neural basis of consciousness remains one of the greatest unsolved mysteries of modern science. The "hard problem" of consciousness, as articulated by philosopher David Chalmers, refers to the fundamental question of how subjective experience arises from the physical processes of the brain—a question that continues to elude even the most sophisticated theories of neural computation.

In our quest to understand the brain mechanisms underlying consciousness, we are confronted with the profound complexity of the human mind—a complexity that defies simple reductionist explanations and invites us to explore the frontiers of cognitive science with humility, curiosity, and wonder.

Section 2: Neurobiological Explanations for Altered States

The exploration of altered states of consciousness offers a unique window into the neurobiological underpinnings of subjective experience, shedding light on the neural mechanisms that govern perception, cognition, and self-awareness. From the profound shifts induced by psychedelic substances to the trance-like states of meditation and hypnosis, altered states challenge our conventional understanding of the mind and invite us to rethink the nature of consciousness itself.

One of the most well-studied altered states is that induced by psychedelic substances such as psilocybin, LSD, and DMT. These compounds exert their effects by binding to serotonin receptors in the brain, particularly those located in the prefrontal cortex and the default mode network—a network of brain regions involved in self-referential thought and introspection. By disrupting the activity of these regions, psychedelics can induce profound alterations in perception, mood, and cognition, leading to experiences of ego dissolution, mystical insight, and profound interconnectedness with the universe.

Similarly, meditation and mindfulness practices have been shown to induce alterations in brain function and structure, leading to changes in attention, emotion regulation, and self-awareness. Functional imaging studies have revealed that experienced meditators exhibit increased activation in regions of the brain associated with attention and emotional regulation, suggesting that these practices may induce lasting changes in the neural circuits underlying consciousness.

Hypnosis represents another fascinating example of an altered state of consciousness that has been the subject of extensive neurobiological investigation. Studies have shown that hypnotic trance is associated with changes in brain activity, including alterations in connectivity between the prefrontal cortex and the limbic system—a network involved in emotional processing and memory retrieval. These findings suggest that hypnosis may involve a temporary reorganization of neural networks, leading to alterations in subjective experience and behavior.

In each of these examples, altered states of consciousness challenge our conventional understanding of the mind-brain relationship, highlighting the dynamic interplay between neural activity and subjective experience. By uncovering the neurobiological mechanisms underlying altered states, we gain valuable insights into the nature of consciousness and the ways in which it can be modulated and transformed.

Yet, for all that we have learned about the neurobiology of altered states, much remains unknown. The subjective nature of consciousness defies simple reductionist explanations, reminding us of the profound mystery that lies at the heart of human experience. As we continue to explore the frontiers of neuroscience, may we approach the study of altered states with open minds and open hearts, ready to embrace the wonders of the mind and the mysteries that lie beyond.

Chapter 4: Meditation and Mindfulness

Section 1: Exploring the Practice of Meditation and Its Effects on Consciousness

Meditation, an ancient practice rooted in contemplative traditions across cultures, has emerged as a powerful tool for exploring the depths of consciousness and cultivating a state of inner peace and clarity. At its core, meditation involves the deliberate cultivation of focused attention and awareness, allowing practitioners to observe the fluctuations of the mind without attachment or judgment.

The practice of meditation takes many forms, ranging from concentration-based techniques such as mindfulness of breath or mantra repetition to insight-oriented practices such as vipassana or Zen meditation. Regardless of the specific technique employed, the underlying principle remains the same: to cultivate a state of present-moment awareness and insight into the nature of reality.

Research has shown that regular meditation practice can lead to a host of cognitive, emotional, and physiological benefits. Studies have demonstrated that meditation can reduce stress and anxiety, enhance emotional regulation, and improve attention and cognitive performance. Moreover, neuroimaging studies have revealed that meditation can induce changes in brain structure and function, leading to alterations in the neural circuits underlying attention, emotion, and self-awareness.

One of the key mechanisms through which meditation exerts its effects on consciousness is through the cultivation of mindfulness—a state of non-judgmental awareness of present-moment experience. By training the mind to observe thoughts, emotions, and sensations with equanimity, practitioners develop greater insight into the nature of their own minds and the impermanent nature of reality itself.

Moreover, meditation offers a unique opportunity to explore altered states of consciousness, from the profound states of concentration and absorption known as jhana in the Buddhist tradition to the experiences of expanded awareness and interconnectedness reported by seasoned meditators. In these states, the boundaries of self and other dissolve, giving rise to feelings of unity, compassion, and transcendence.

In essence, meditation serves as a gateway to the depths of consciousness, inviting practitioners to explore the inner landscape of the mind with curiosity, compassion, and humility. By cultivating a state of present-moment awareness, meditation offers a path to liberation from the cycles of suffering and delusion that perpetuate human existence, leading to greater clarity, insight, and inner peace.

Section 2: Mindfulness Techniques and Their Impact on Altering Perception

Mindfulness, a core aspect of many meditation practices, involves the cultivation of non-judgmental awareness and acceptance of present-moment experience. Rooted in Buddhist philosophy, mindfulness has been adapted into secular contexts as a therapeutic intervention for a wide range of psychological and emotional disorders, from depression and anxiety to chronic pain and addiction.

One of the key techniques used to cultivate mindfulness is the practice of mindful breathing, in which practitioners focus their attention on the sensations of the breath as it moves in and out of the body. By anchoring the mind in the present moment, mindful breathing helps to quiet the chatter of the thinking mind and bring attention back to the here and now.

Another common mindfulness technique is body scan meditation, in which practitioners systematically scan through the body, bringing attention to each area and observing any sensations or tensions that arise. This practice helps to cultivate greater awareness of bodily sensations and promotes relaxation and stress reduction.

Mindfulness-based stress reduction (MBSR) and mindfulness-based cognitive therapy (MBCT) are two structured programs that integrate mindfulness practices with cognitive-behavioral techniques to promote psychological well-being and emotional resilience. These programs have been shown to be effective in reducing symptoms of depression, anxiety, and chronic pain, and have been widely adopted in clinical settings around the world.

The impact of mindfulness techniques on altering perception extends beyond the realm of clinical psychology to encompass broader aspects of human experience. By cultivating present-moment awareness, mindfulness allows individuals to see the world with fresh eyes, free from the distortions of past conditioning and future projections. It encourages a sense of openness, curiosity, and wonder, inviting practitioners to explore the richness and complexity of the present moment with clarity and receptivity.

Moreover, mindfulness techniques can enhance our capacity for empathy and compassion, fostering a deeper connection with ourselves and others. By attuning to the inner workings of the mind and heart, mindfulness cultivates a sense of empathy and understanding towards the suffering of others, fostering a more compassionate and inclusive society.

In conclusion, the practice of meditation and mindfulness offers a transformative path to self-discovery and personal growth. By exploring the depths of consciousness and altering perception, practitioners can cultivate greater clarity, insight, and compassion in their lives, leading to greater fulfillment, well-being, and harmony with the world around them. As we continue to explore the profound implications of meditation and mindfulness, may we embrace these ancient practices with open hearts and open minds, recognizing their potential to awaken us to the boundless depths of human consciousness.

Chapter 5: Psychedelics and Altered Consciousness

Section 1: Historical Context and Modern Resurgence of Psychedelic Research.

The exploration of psychedelics and their effects on consciousness traces back millennia, woven into the fabric of human history through rituals, ceremonies, and spiritual practices. Indigenous cultures around the world have long utilized psychedelic substances such as psilocybin mushrooms, peyote, and ayahuasca as sacraments in sacred rituals and healing ceremonies, honoring the profound role these substances play in expanding consciousness and facilitating spiritual insight.

In the mid-20th century, psychedelics burst onto the Western cultural scene, catalyzing a paradigm shift in the fields of psychology, psychiatry, and neuroscience. Pioneering researchers such as Albert Hofmann, Timothy Leary, and Stanislav Grof conducted groundbreaking studies on the effects of psychedelics, exploring their potential for therapeutic healing, spiritual growth, and consciousness expansion.

However, the widespread recreational use of psychedelics during the countercultural revolution of the 1960s prompted a backlash from government authorities, leading to their criminalization and stigmatization as dangerous drugs with no legitimate medical use. As a result, research into the therapeutic potential of psychedelics ground to a halt, relegating these powerful substances to the fringes of society for decades.

In recent years, however, there has been a remarkable resurgence of interest in psychedelics as tools for therapeutic healing and scientific inquiry. Pioneering studies conducted at institutions such as Johns Hopkins University, Imperial College London, and the Multidisciplinary Association for Psychedelic Studies (MAPS) have provided compelling evidence for the efficacy of psychedelics in treating a range of mental health disorders, including depression, anxiety, PTSD, and addiction.

The resurgence of psychedelic research has been fueled by a growing recognition of the limitations of conventional psychiatric treatments and a renewed openness to alternative approaches to healing and consciousness exploration. Advances in neuroimaging technology have allowed researchers to peer into the brain and observe the effects of psychedelics on neural activity, shedding light on the mechanisms underlying their therapeutic effects and altered states of consciousness.

Moreover, shifting cultural attitudes towards psychedelics have paved the way for a reevaluation of their potential benefits and risks. A growing number of voices within the scientific community, as well as mainstream media outlets and public figures, have called for the decriminalization and legalization of psychedelics, recognizing their potential to revolutionize mental healthcare and catalyze transformative shifts in consciousness.

The resurgence of psychedelic research represents a profound change in basic assumptions in our understanding of consciousness and mental health—a shift towards a more holistic and integrative approach to healing that honors the profound interconnectedness of mind, body, and spirit. As we continue to explore the therapeutic potential of psychedelics, may we do so with reverence, respect, and a commitment to fostering greater understanding and compassion for ourselves and the world around us.

Section 2: Effects of Psychedelics on Perception, Cognition, and Consciousness.

The effects of psychedelics on perception, cognition, and consciousness are as profound as they are multifaceted, offering a window into the boundless depths of human experience and the mysteries of the mind. At the heart of the psychedelic experience lies a profound sense of dissolution of the ego—a transcendence of the self that opens the door to states of expanded awareness, unity, and interconnectedness with the cosmos.

One of the hallmark effects of psychedelics is the alteration of perception, characterized by vivid hallucinations, synesthesia, and enhanced sensory perception. Colors may appear more vibrant, music more profound, and ordinary objects may take on a surreal and otherworldly quality. Time may appear to slow down or dissolve altogether, leading to a sense of timelessness and eternity.

Psychedelics also exert profound effects on cognition, leading to alterations in thought patterns, beliefs, and self-perception. Users may experience a dissolution of boundaries between the self and the external world, leading to feelings of unity and interconnectedness with all of creation. This sense of ego dissolution can be both terrifying and liberating, opening the door to profound insights and spiritual awakenings.

Moreover, psychedelics have been shown to induce states of profound altered consciousness, characterized by a sense of interconnectedness, awe, and reverence for the mysteries of existence. Users may experience a sense of merging with the universe, transcending the limitations of the individual self and tapping into a deeper wellspring of wisdom and insight.

Recent research has shed light on the neurobiological mechanisms underlying the effects of psychedelics on perception, cognition, and consciousness. Studies have shown that psychedelics such as psilocybin and LSD exert their effects primarily through agonism of serotonin receptors in the brain, particularly the 5-HT2A receptor subtype. Activation of these receptors leads to changes in neural activity and connectivity, disrupting default mode network activity and promoting the emergence of altered states of consciousness.

The therapeutic potential of psychedelics lies in their ability to facilitate profound shifts in consciousness and promote healing at the deepest levels of the psyche. Studies have shown that psychedelics can induce powerful mystical experiences characterized by feelings of unity, transcendence, and ineffability—a phenomenon that has been linked to lasting improvements in psychological well-being and quality of life.

In conclusion, the effects of psychedelics on perception, cognition, and consciousness offer a profound window into the mysteries of the human mind and the nature of reality itself. By challenging our perceptions of self and world, psychedelics invite us to explore the depths of consciousness with humility, reverence, and awe. As we continue to unlock the therapeutic potential of psychedelics, may we do so with wisdom, compassion, and a deep respect for the profound mysteries of existence.

Chapter 6: Dreams and Lucid Dreaming

Section 1: The Nature of Dreams and Their Role in Altered States.

Dreams have fascinated and mystified humanity since time immemorial, serving as portals to realms of the unconscious mind and windows into the depths of human experience. Defined as a succession of images, thoughts, emotions, and sensations that occur involuntarily during sleep, dreams offer a rich tapestry of symbolic imagery and narrative themes that reflect the inner workings of the psyche.

The nature of dreams is inherently elusive, shrouded in mystery and subject to interpretation. Throughout history, dreams have been imbued with profound significance, serving as sources of divine revelation, prophetic insight, and psychological exploration. In ancient cultures, dreams were revered as messages from the gods, offering guidance, warnings, and glimpses into the future. In modern psychology, dreams are viewed as reflections of unconscious desires, fears, and conflicts—a window into the hidden recesses of the mind.

Dreams play a pivotal role in altered states of consciousness, blurring the boundaries between waking reality and the realm of the subconscious mind. During sleep, the brain undergoes a series of complex neurological processes that give rise to the phenomenon of dreaming. Rapid eye movement (REM) sleep, characterized by heightened brain activity and vivid dreaming, is thought to play a particularly significant role in the consolidation of memories, emotional processing, and creative problem-solving.

Moreover, dreams have been linked to altered states of consciousness, including lucid dreaming, sleep paralysis, and out-of-body experiences. In these states, the boundaries of perception and reality become blurred, giving rise to experiences that defy conventional explanation and challenge our understanding of the nature of consciousness itself.

In essence, dreams serve as portals to the depths of the human psyche, offering insights into the innermost workings of the mind and the mysteries of existence. By exploring the nature of dreams and their role in altered states of consciousness, we gain a deeper appreciation for the complexity and richness of human experience, and the vast potential of the unconscious mind.

Section 2: Techniques for Achieving Lucid Dreaming and Its Implications for Consciousness.

Lucid dreaming, a phenomenon in which the dreamer becomes aware of the fact that they are dreaming while still immersed in the dream state, represents a profound opportunity for exploring the depths of consciousness and harnessing the power of the unconscious mind. In a lucid dream, the dreamer retains a sense of self-awareness and agency, allowing them to actively participate in and even manipulate the dream environment.

The practice of lucid dreaming dates back centuries, with references to conscious dreaming found in ancient texts and traditions from around the world. In Tibetan Buddhism, for example, practitioners engage in dream yoga—a form of meditation aimed at cultivating awareness and control within the dream state. Similarly, Indigenous cultures have long recognized the potential of lucid dreaming as a means of accessing spiritual insight and guidance.

Modern techniques for achieving lucid dreaming include reality testing, mnemonic induction of lucid dreams (MILD), wake-induced lucid dreaming (WILD), and the use of external cues such as dream journals and reality checks. Reality testing involves regularly questioning one's state of consciousness throughout the day, asking oneself whether one is dreaming or awake. By cultivating a habit of mindfulness and self-awareness, individuals increase their chances of recognizing the dream state when it occurs.

Mnemonic induction of lucid dreams (MILD) involves setting intentions before sleep to become lucid within the dream state. By repeating affirmations and visualizing oneself becoming lucid, individuals create a mental framework that primes the mind for awareness and self-reflection during sleep.

Wake-induced lucid dreaming (WILD) involves maintaining awareness while transitioning from wakefulness to sleep, allowing individuals to enter the dream state consciously and with intention. By remaining in a state of relaxed attentiveness, individuals can navigate the threshold between waking reality and the dream world, facilitating lucidity and self-directed exploration.

The implications of lucid dreaming for consciousness are profound, offering a unique opportunity to explore the boundaries of perception, reality, and selfhood. By cultivating awareness within the dream state, individuals gain insights into the nature of consciousness itself, questioning the fundamental assumptions that underlie waking reality and opening the door to new possibilities for personal growth and self-discovery.

Moreover, lucid dreaming has practical applications for enhancing creativity, problem-solving, and emotional well-being. By engaging with the symbolic imagery and narrative themes of dreams, individuals gain access to a vast reservoir of unconscious wisdom and insight, unlocking the creative potential of the mind and fostering greater resilience and adaptability in the face of life's challenges.

In conclusion, lucid dreaming represents a powerful tool for exploring the depths of consciousness and unlocking the hidden potentials of the human mind. By embracing the practice of lucid dreaming, individuals can tap into the transformative power of the unconscious, harnessing its creative energies and expanding the horizons of human experience. As we continue to explore the mysteries of lucid dreaming and its implications for consciousness, may we do so with open minds and open hearts, ready to embark on a journey of self-discovery and spiritual awakening.

Chapter 7: Altered States in Shamanic Traditions

Section 1: Examination of Shamanic Practices and Their Use of Altered States

Shamanic traditions represent some of the oldest and most enduring spiritual practices known to humanity, spanning cultures and continents across the globe. At the heart of shamanism lies the shaman—a spiritual practitioner endowed with the ability to journey between the realms of the seen and the unseen, serving as a mediator between the human and spirit worlds.

Central to shamanic practice is the induction of altered states of consciousness, achieved through various techniques such as drumming, chanting, dancing, and the use of psychoactive plants. These altered states serve as gateways to the spirit world, allowing shamans to communicate with ancestors, spirits, and other non-human entities for healing, guidance, and insight.

Drumming is perhaps the most widely used technique for inducing altered states in shamanic practice. The rhythmic beat of the drum serves as a powerful tool for altering brainwave patterns and facilitating trance states, enabling the shaman to enter into a state of expanded awareness and receptivity. Through the repetitive rhythm of the drum, shamans are able to journey beyond the confines of ordinary perception and access the hidden realms of the unconscious mind.

Chanting and singing are also common methods used to induce altered states in shamanic rituals. The repetitive chanting of sacred songs and mantras creates a resonance that reverberates throughout the body, altering consciousness and opening the doors of perception to the mysteries of the spirit world. By harmonizing with the rhythms of creation, shamans are able to attune themselves to the vibrational frequencies of the cosmos, allowing for profound experiences of unity and connection.

The use of psychoactive plants, such as ayahuasca, peyote, and iboga, is another hallmark of shamanic practice. These sacred plants contain powerful psychoactive compounds that alter brain chemistry and induce altered states of consciousness characterized by vivid visions, profound insights, and spiritual revelations. Through the ingestion of these plants, shamans are able to transcend the limitations of the ego and commune with the divine forces that animate the universe.

In shamanic cultures, altered states are not merely seen as subjective experiences, but as portals to deeper truths and higher dimensions of reality. Shamans serve as mediators between the human and spirit worlds, navigating the unseen realms with wisdom, courage, and humility. Through their journeys into altered states, shamans seek to heal the sick, restore balance to the community, and maintain harmony with the natural world.

Section 2: Cultural and Spiritual Significance of Shamanic Journeys.

The practice of shamanism is deeply rooted in the cultural and spiritual traditions of Indigenous peoples around the world, reflecting a profound reverence for the natural world and a deep understanding of the interconnectedness of all life. Shamanic journeys serve as a means of accessing the wisdom of the ancestors, communing with the spirits of the land, and honoring the sacred cycles of birth, death, and rebirth.

In many shamanic cultures, the role of the shaman is not merely that of a healer or spiritual guide, but of a custodian of ancestral wisdom and guardian of the community. Shamans undergo rigorous training and initiation rites to prepare them for their role as intermediaries between the human and spirit worlds, learning ancient chants, rituals, and healing techniques passed down through generations.

The cultural and spiritual significance of shamanic journeys extends beyond individual healing to encompass broader social, ecological, and cosmological dimensions. Shamans serve as stewards of the land, advocating for environmental conservation and promoting sustainable ways of living in harmony with nature. They also play a vital role in maintaining social cohesion and resolving conflicts within the community, serving as mediators and peacemakers in times of crisis.

Shamanic journeys are often marked by profound encounters with spirits, ancestors, and other non-human entities that inhabit the unseen realms. These encounters serve as opportunities for learning, growth, and transformation, offering insights into the mysteries of existence and the nature of reality itself. Through their journeys, shamans gain a deeper understanding of the interconnected web of life and their place within it, fostering a sense of reverence, gratitude, and awe for the sacredness of all creation.

In conclusion, the practice of shamanism offers a profound and deeply rooted approach to exploring altered states of consciousness and accessing the hidden dimensions of reality. Through their rituals, ceremonies, and journeys, shamans serve as bridges between the human and spirit worlds, offering healing, guidance, and wisdom to those in need. As we continue to explore the cultural and spiritual significance of shamanic traditions, may we honor the ancient wisdom of the shamans and embrace the interconnectedness of all life with humility, reverence, and gratitude.

Chapter 8: Technological Alterations of Consciousness

In the modern era, the intersection of technology and consciousness represents a fascinating frontier of exploration. Rapid advancements in technology have provided humanity with tools and platforms to alter, augment, and even transcend traditional modes of consciousness. From virtual reality (VR) simulations to brain-computer interfaces (BCIs), the impact of technology on altering consciousness is profound and multifaceted, offering both opportunities for enhancement and challenges for ethical consideration.

Section 1: The Impact of Technology on Altering Consciousness.

Technology has a profound impact on altering consciousness by shaping the way we perceive, interpret, and interact with the world around us. Through the omnipresence of digital devices, social media platforms, and immersive experiences, technology has become an integral part of our daily lives, influencing our thoughts, behaviors, and relationships in profound ways.

One of the primary ways technology alters consciousness is through the manipulation of attention and cognition. The constant barrage of notifications, alerts, and stimuli from digital devices can lead to fragmented attention and diminished capacity for deep focus and concentration. As a result, our perception of time, space, and self may become distorted, leading to a sense of disconnection and alienation from the present moment.

Moreover, technology has the power to shape our beliefs, values, and worldview through the dissemination of information and the propagation of narratives. Social media algorithms, search engine algorithms, and recommendation systems filter and curate the content we consume, shaping our understanding of reality and influencing our attitudes and behaviors in subtle ways. This phenomenon, known as filter bubbles and echo chambers, can lead to the polarization of society and the reinforcement of pre-existing biases and prejudices.

Virtual reality (VR) represents a groundbreaking technology that has the potential to radically alter our perception of reality and consciousness. By creating immersive digital environments that simulate sensory inputs such as vision, hearing, and touch, VR can transport users to virtual worlds that are indistinguishable from physical reality. Through the manipulation of sensory stimuli and environmental cues, VR can induce altered states of consciousness characterized by a sense of presence, immersion, and embodiment.

Brain-computer interfaces (BCIs) offer another avenue for altering consciousness by enabling direct communication between the brain and external devices. BCIs decode neural signals generated by the brain and translate them into actionable commands that can be used to control computers, prosthetic limbs, and other devices. By bypassing traditional modes of input and output, BCIs have the potential to enhance human capabilities and augment our cognitive and perceptual faculties in unprecedented ways.

Section 2: Virtual Reality, Brain-Computer Interfaces, and Their Potential Effects on Perception and Reality.

Virtual reality (VR) and brain-computer interfaces (BCIs) represent two innovative technologies that have the potential to reshape our perception of reality and alter the landscape of human consciousness.

VR technology immerses users in computer-generated environments that simulate sensory inputs such as vision, hearing, and touch, creating a sense of presence and immersion in virtual worlds. By simulating sensory inputs and environmental cues, VR has the ability to induce altered states of consciousness characterized by a sense of presence and immersion in the virtual environment.

The potential effects of VR on perception and reality are far-reaching, encompassing both therapeutic applications and recreational experiences. In the realm of mental health, VR has shown promise as a tool for exposure therapy, allowing individuals to confront and overcome phobias, PTSD, and other anxiety-related disorders in a safe and controlled environment. VR-based interventions have also been used to treat chronic pain, addiction, and neurodevelopmental disorders, offering new hope for those struggling with debilitating conditions.

On the recreational front, VR has revolutionized the entertainment industry, offering immersive gaming experiences, interactive storytelling, and virtual social environments where users can connect and interact with others from around the world. From exploring ancient ruins to traversing distant galaxies, VR transports users to realms of imagination and possibility previously reserved for the realm of science fiction.

Brain-computer interfaces (BCIs) represent another frontier in the quest to alter consciousness and enhance human capabilities. BCIs enable direct communication between the brain and external devices, allowing users to control computers, prosthetic limbs, and other devices using nothing but their thoughts. By decoding neural activity and translating it into actionable commands, BCIs offer new avenues for human-computer interaction and provide a lifeline for individuals with severe motor impairments.

The potential applications of BCIs extend far beyond assistive technology to encompass cognitive enhancement, neurofeedback, and brain-to-brain communication. Researchers are exploring the use of BCIs to augment learning and memory, optimize cognitive performance, and facilitate communication between individuals with locked-in syndrome and their caregivers. BCIs also hold promise for restoring sensory perception to those with sensory impairments, such as blindness or deafness, by bypassing damaged sensory organs and directly stimulating the brain's neural circuits.

In conclusion, the impact of technology on consciousness is both profound and multifaceted, offering new possibilities for exploration, self-expression, and human connection. As we harness the power of VR and BCIs to alter our perception of reality, may we do so with wisdom, compassion, and a deep respect for the mysteries of the human mind and the boundless potential of human consciousness.

Chapter 9: The Philosophy of Consciousness

Exploring the philosophy of consciousness delves into the fundamental questions about the nature of reality, the mind, and our subjective experiences. This chapter traverses the rich tapestry of philosophical perspectives on consciousness and reality, contemplating the metaphysical implications of altered states and their philosophical interpretations.

Section 1: Philosophical Perspectives on Consciousness and Reality.

Philosophy has long grappled with the enigma of consciousness, seeking to unravel its mysteries and understand its place in the universe. From ancient Greek philosophy to contemporary debates in analytic and continental philosophy, the nature of consciousness has been a central focus of philosophical inquiry.

One of the oldest philosophical perspectives on consciousness is dualism, which posits that consciousness is fundamentally distinct from the physical world and cannot be reduced to material processes. This view, championed by philosophers such as René Descartes, suggests that consciousness possesses unique properties that cannot be explained solely in terms of brain activity or neural processes.

In contrast, monism holds that consciousness is an emergent property of physical processes and is ultimately reducible to the workings of the brain. Materialist and physicalist philosophies subscribe to this view, asserting that consciousness arises from the complex interactions of neurons, synapses, and neural networks in the brain.

Idealist philosophies, on the other hand, propose that consciousness is primary, and that the physical world is a manifestation or projection of consciousness itself. From the Vedanta philosophy of ancient India to the idealism of philosophers like George Berkeley, idealism challenges the notion of an objective, external reality independent of consciousness.

Existentialist and phenomenological philosophies offer yet another perspective on consciousness, emphasizing the subjective nature of experience and the role of consciousness in shaping our perceptions of reality. Existentialist thinkers such as Jean-Paul Sartre and Martin Heidegger explore the existential dimensions of consciousness, grappling with questions of meaning, authenticity, and freedom in the face of existential angst and uncertainty.

Phenomenology, pioneered by philosophers like Edmund Husserl and Maurice Merleau-Ponty, investigates the structures of consciousness and the ways in which we experience the world through subjective phenomena such as perception, intentionality, and embodiment.

Ultimately, the philosophical perspectives on consciousness and reality reflect the diverse ways in which human beings have grappled with the mystery of existence and sought to make sense of their place in the cosmos. Whether through dualism, monism, idealism, existentialism, or phenomenology, philosophy invites us to contemplate the nature of consciousness with humility, curiosity, and wonder.

Section 2: Metaphysical Implications of Altered States and Their Philosophical Interpretations.

Altered states of consciousness offer profound insights into the nature of reality and the metaphysical dimensions of human experience. From mystical states of union and transcendence to psychedelic experiences of expanded awareness and interconnectedness, altered states challenge our conventional understanding of reality and invite us to explore the depths of consciousness with open minds and open hearts.

One of the central metaphysical implications of altered states is the dissolution of the ego—the sense of individual identity and separateness that defines our everyday experience of reality. In altered states, the boundaries between self and other, subject and object, dissolve, giving rise to feelings of unity, interconnectedness, and oneness with the cosmos.

This dissolution of egoic boundaries has profound implications for our understanding of consciousness and the nature of reality. From a metaphysical perspective, altered states suggest that consciousness is not confined to the individual mind or brain but is a fundamental aspect of the fabric of the universe itself. In this view, consciousness is not something we possess but something we participate in—a cosmic dance of awareness unfolding through time and space.

Moreover, altered states challenge our notions of linear time and causality, opening the door to experiences of timelessness, eternity, and synchronicity. In states of expanded awareness, the past, present, and future collapse into an eternal now, and the veil of linear time is lifted, revealing the interconnected web of existence in all its intricate beauty and complexity.

Altered states also raise profound questions about the nature of reality and the relationship between the subjective and objective dimensions of experience. In psychedelic experiences, for example, individuals may encounter visions, archetypal symbols, and mythic narratives that transcend the boundaries of ordinary perception and point to deeper truths about the nature of existence.

From a philosophical perspective, altered states challenge us to reevaluate our assumptions about reality and to adopt a more expansive view of consciousness and its potentialities. Rather than seeing consciousness as a byproduct of brain activity or neural processes, altered states suggest that consciousness is the ground of being—the creative force that animates the cosmos and gives rise to the myriad forms and phenomena of existence.

In conclusion, the metaphysical implications of altered states invite us to rethink our understanding of consciousness and reality and to explore the depths of human experience with humility, curiosity, and reverence. Whether through philosophy, mysticism, or scientific inquiry, the exploration of altered states opens doors to new dimensions of understanding and invites us to embrace the mystery of existence with open minds and open hearts.

Chapter 10: Integration and Future Directions

The concluding chapter of "Consciousness and Altered States: Exploring the Depths of Perception and Reality" serves as a bridge between theory and practice, exploring strategies for integrating insights from altered states into everyday life while navigating the ethical considerations that accompany consciousness studies.

Section 1: Strategies for Integrating Insights from Altered States into Everyday Life.

Altered states of consciousness offer profound insights and transformative experiences that can enrich our lives and deepen our understanding of reality. However, the challenge lies in integrating these insights into our everyday existence and translating them into meaningful action and personal growth.

One strategy for integration is the cultivation of mindfulness and self-awareness in daily life. By developing a regular meditation practice and cultivating present-moment awareness, individuals can learn to observe their thoughts, emotions, and sensations with nonjudgmental attention, gaining insight into the workings of their minds and the nature of consciousness itself.

Mindfulness practices such as breath awareness, body scanning, and loving-kindness meditation can help individuals cultivate inner peace, resilience, and emotional well-being in the face of life's challenges. By bringing awareness to the present moment and cultivating a sense of inner spaciousness, individuals can navigate the difficulties of life with greater ease and equanimity.

Another strategy for integration is the exploration of somatic practices and embodied awareness. Embodied practices such as yoga, tai chi, and qigong offer powerful tools for connecting with the wisdom of the body and accessing deeper levels of consciousness. By tuning into the sensations, movements, and rhythms of the body, individuals can cultivate a sense of groundedness, vitality, and aliveness that nourishes the mind, body, and spirit.

Creative expression is another avenue for integrating insights from altered states into everyday life. Through art, music, dance, and other forms of creative expression, individuals can give voice to the ineffable dimensions of consciousness and explore the mysteries of existence in ways that transcend language and rational thought. Creativity allows for the expression of the soul and the integration of the unconscious mind, fostering a sense of wholeness and authenticity in the creative process.

Community and social connection play a vital role in the integration of altered states into everyday life. By connecting with like-minded individuals and participating in conscious communities, individuals can share their experiences, insights, and challenges in a supportive and nurturing environment. Through dialogue, collaboration, and mutual support, individuals can deepen their understanding of consciousness and co-create a more conscious and compassionate world.

Section 2: Ethical Considerations in Consciousness Studies.

Ethical consciousness studies are essential for navigating the complex terrain of altered states and ensuring that research and practice are conducted with integrity, compassion, and respect for the dignity and autonomy of all beings.

One ethical consideration is the importance of informed consent in consciousness research and practice. Individuals participating in research studies or therapeutic sessions involving altered states must be fully informed about the potential risks, benefits, and alternatives to participation. Informed consent requires transparency, honesty, and respect for the individual's right to make autonomous decisions about their own consciousness and well-being.

Another ethical consideration is the need for responsible and sustainable use of psychoactive substances in consciousness research and therapy. While psychedelics and other psychoactive substances hold tremendous therapeutic potential, they also carry risks and uncertainties that must be carefully considered and managed. Researchers and practitioners have a responsibility to uphold rigorous safety protocols, minimize potential harms, and prioritize the well-being of participants primarily.

Cultural sensitivity and respect for Indigenous wisdom and traditions are also essential ethical considerations in consciousness studies. Many of the practices and substances used to induce altered states have deep roots in Indigenous cultures and spiritual traditions, and it is essential to honor and respect the cultural heritage and intellectual property rights of Indigenous peoples. Researchers and practitioners must collaborate with Indigenous communities, seek their input and guidance, and ensure that their voices are heard and respected in all aspects of consciousness research and practice.

Finally, ethical consciousness studies require a commitment to social justice, equity, and inclusivity in all aspects of research, education, and practice. Consciousness studies have historically been dominated by white, male, Western perspectives, and there is a need for greater diversity, representation, and inclusion within the field. Researchers and practitioners must actively work to dismantle systems of oppression and privilege, challenge institutional barriers to access and inclusion, and create spaces that honor and celebrate the diversity of human experience.

In conclusion, integration and future directions in consciousness studies require a holistic approach that encompasses both personal transformation and collective evolution. By cultivating mindfulness, embodied awareness, creativity, community, and ethical consciousness, individuals and societies can harness the transformative power of altered states to create a more conscious, compassionate, and sustainable world for future generations.

www.ingramcontent.com/pod-product-compliance
Lightning Source LLC
Chambersburg PA
CBHW051713250726
48653CB00007B/3008